LOTTIE MOON OF CHINA

LOTTIE MOON OF CHINA

JESTER SUMMERS
Illustrated by James Ponter

BROADMAN PRESS
Nashville, Tennessee

Dewey Decimal Classification Number: J266.092
Library of Congress Catalog Card Number: 70-117304
Printed in the United States of America
15.Jy7018

1571083

Contents

1
The New Baby

Smoke poured from the huge chimneys of the Viewmont great-house. Inside, it was as warm as all the fireplaces could make it, for this was a special day!

Upstairs in Mother's bedroom, a new baby girl had just been born. The father, Mr. Edward Harris Moon, proudly told the good news to each member of the plantation household.

"What have you named her?" they wanted to know.

"Charlotte Diggs," explained the father. "We have given her my mother's name."

Before the day was over, Mr. Moon

took his two older children, Thomas and Oriana, to see the tiny newcomer.

"When she grows a little," Father told them, "you will have another play-mate."

Father then went downstairs to his desk in the front hall. He opened a large Bible to the center pages where family births, marriages, and deaths were re-corded. Just below the records of Thomas and Oriana he wrote:

born: *Charlotte Diggs Moon*
December 12, 1840

to: *Edward and Anna Maria Moon*

at: *Viewmont Plantation*
Albemarle County, Virginia

2
Lottie Learns to Make Cookies

The front hall door of the great-house at Viewmont flew open. In raced a little girl with her shepherd dog. Down the long hall they dashed, into the dining room, around the table, into the library, and back into the dining room.

"Whoa, Miss Lottie," exclaimed a friendly looking man who was carrying a large covered platter to the table. "You'll make me spill this fried chicken and ham. Then what would your mother serve her company for dinner?"

"Oh, you could think of something, I'm sure," was Lottie's quick answer.

Just then the "wash-up-before-dinner" bell rang loud and clear.

Charlotte Diggs Moon, now called Lottie, stopped dead-still. She turned and put her pet outside. Then she ran to her room where Mandy sat rocking.

"Mandy, will you smooth my hair and help me wash my face and hands in a hurry?" Lottie asked. "Mother really means for me to obey that bell. Do you remember the last time I was late for a meal?"

"Yes," replied Mandy. "You had to

come to your room and eat bread and milk."

"I know. And downstairs they had everything I liked plus my favorite— blackberry cobbler."

Mandy finished smoothing the shiny brown hair. She inspected Lottie's hands and face and said, "There! You look just right. Your mother will be proud of you."

Lottie gave Mandy a hug and dashed for the head of the stairs. But once there she primly went down the steps just as she had often watched her mother do.

As she reached the downstairs hall, she saw Mother and Father talking with a strange woman.

"Lottie," Father said, "this is your schoolteacher. She will live here at Viewmont. She will help you learn to read, write, do arithmetic, and study music."

Lottie curtsied in the way a young girl greeted an older person. Inside she was

excited. She thought, "I am going to learn all those things. I will like that!"

After the meal, Mrs. Moon spoke to Lottie and Oriana. "I have not forgotten my promise to help you make cookies," she said. "I will have time this afternoon. Meet me in the kitchen in an hour."

Lottie began to clap her hands and jump up and down. "Yum, yum!" she exclaimed. "I love Mother's cookies."

Within the hour both girls were skipping through the halls, out the side door, and down the walk to the kitchen. The family cooking was done in a small, separate house to the side and back of the main home.

It was not long before Mother came with a basket of large keys in her hand.

"First, we must get the supplies we will need," she explained. "Bring the bowls from the table and come with me to the storage room."

Mrs. Moon took a key from her basket and unlocked a door in one end of the long kitchen. Lottie and Oriana followed. Inside the room they saw huge bins and barrels, churns and crockery jars.

Mother took out another key and opened the largest bin. "Fill your bowls with flour," she directed, "but be careful not to spill any. It must last us all winter."

She then unlocked a smaller bin from

which the girls took the right amount of loaf sugar. The bins were relocked, and the three went back into the kitchen with their supplies.

"We must go to the springhouse next for eggs, butter, and milk," Mother decided. And out they went, down the hill to a wooded place where there was another little house.

"I like to come here," Lottie said as Mother turned the key in the lock. "It's always so cool inside."

With Mother's help the girls collected what they needed. Before they left, they took a dipper from the springhouse wall and drank the cold, clear water that bubbled out from between smooth, clean rocks.

As they reached the kitchen, they found Thomas Moon helping Sam, the cook's son. The two were adding wood to the kitchen fires. "Thank you, boys," Mother said. "That will be wood enough

to make a very hot oven for all the cookies we'll bake today."

"May we stay and help?" Thomas
begged.

"You know boys don't cook!" Lottie
replied.

"Oh, all right," Thomas mumbled as
he left. Now and then Thomas and Sam
came near the kitchen door just to see
whether or not the cookies were ready to
eat.

Inside the kitchen Mother showed

15

each girl how to break an egg and beat it. Then she guided them to weigh ½ pound of flour (measures 2 cups), ¼ pound of butter (measures a little more than ½ cup butter), ¼ pound of loaf sugar (measures a heaping cup of sugar when granulated), 1 egg well beaten, and 1 tablespoon of cream. She helped them grate the sugar and cream it into the soft butter.

"Now mix these ingredients into the beaten egg, add the flour, and 1 table-spoon of cream," she directed. When this was done, Mrs. Moon let them dust flour on separate boards, and on their hands, too.

"Put the dough on the floured board. Roll it out very thin with rolling pins," Mother continued. "Now cut it with a water glass and place the cookies on these buttered iron pans."

The sisters followed Mother's sugges-tions. Then they placed the pans of

cookies in the very hot oven to cook for about five minutes. *

When all the cookies were done, Mother poured milk, and the three cooks sat down to enjoy what they had made.

"These are good!" Lottie exclaimed. "They taste a little like yours, Mother."

* If you wish to make the cookies on page 16, follow the directions for mixing, but do not roll them out. Drop them far apart on a cookie pan. Oven should be about 475°. These cookies need no baking powder. They were called sugar biscuits.

"You have done well this first time," Mother replied. "We will make them often until you can bake them as well as I can."

"And you may give Thomas and Sam several now for here they come." She got up to pour two more glasses of milk.

That evening Lottie said to Oriana, "Just think! We can make cookies anytime we want to as soon as we learn to do it all by ourselves. I'm going to make them for the rest of my life. I like them just that much!"

3
Snowtime and
Storytime

"Wake up, sleepyhead," Mandy whispered as she gently patted the form doubled up under the downy cover.

"I don't want to wake up yet, Mandy. It's warm under here."

"Wake up and see what has happened outside," Mandy coaxed.

The covers flew back and out jumped Lottie. "Has it snowed?" she shouted as she dashed to the window. "It has! It has! Help me get dressed fast, please, Mandy."

And in half the time it usually took, she was dressed. Down the stairs she ran, and rushed from one window to another to see the white snow glistening in the sun.

After breakfast Mr. Moon announced, "Children, since this is the first snow of the year, you need not have school to-day."

"Thank you, Father!" they all said at once. And they soon finished their meal.

Lottie and the others put on their coats, caps, boots, and gloves, and hurried outside to play. Now and then they dashed into the kitchen to warm their

toes and drink a hot cup of milk. Other times they went into the great-house to rest awhile.

About mid-afternoon Father called "It is time to come in now. The sun is getting low, and it's too cold to stay out longer. Tomorrow after classes you may play again."

Then he added as the children started slowly to the house, "Mother has a hot snack for you in her room. She will read to you as soon as you have changed your clothes."

"Whoo-pee!" they all shouted as they began to run for the house.

They dressed quickly and went down the hall to Mother's sitting room. As they reached the door, they heard her say, "Come in and warm yourselves here before the fire."

She served them hot apple cider and ham biscuits. When they had finished eating and were warm, she opened a

brand new book and began to read. The story was about the Judsons, a young man and his wife, who went across the ocean to be missionaries in Burma, a country near India. The people there had never even heard of Jesus.

Lottie grew so interested in all the things that happened to the Judsons, that she begged Mother to read on even when the supper bell rang. "I'll read to you again tomorrow," Mother promised.

After that, anytime Mother read from

the new book, Lottie sat as still as a mouse.

"It must be wonderful to go to a foreign land," Lottie told her mother after hearing the whole story.

"Yes, my child, it is." Then Mother added, "But it's more wonderful to go as the Judsons did—as missionaries."

4
Sabbath Smoke
from the
Kitchen Chimney

It was Saturday at Viewmont.

In the kitchen the cooks were busy roasting a ham, frying chickens, and baking bread for Sunday.

The maids were making the great-house extra clean. Out in the laundry shed, women were washing clothes and ironing.

Mrs. Moon was going to and from the kitchen, the laundry, and the great-house to see that everything was being readied for the "sabbath."

No work, not even cooking, was allowed at Viewmont on that day. "Remember the sabbath to keep it holy," quoted Mrs. Moon. "And that is a sensible law," she explained. "Everyone needs one day out of seven to rest and think about God."

"But I don't need any rest, and I think about God everyday," thought Lottie. "I like Saturday best. Then I can play hide-and-seek, climb trees, race up and down the hills, pick flowers from the garden, or do whatever I want."

And she continued to think of why Saturday was such a good time of the week. "I can watch Flo and the others scrub the clothes on the washboard and hear them sing about heaven as they do. But on Sunday I have to dress up and ride in the carriage all the way to Scottsville. I can't even stop once along the way to pick wild berries."

Her thoughts kept running on. "And we always eat a cold dinner when we get home. That is the worst part of it all!" Lottie was always hungry at this age.

On one particular Saturday following the death of her father some months before, Lottie, now twelve years old, said very little and sat around for most of the day.

At breakfast the next morning Mother noticed that Lottie was still silent. "Are you sick, my dear?" she asked.

"No, Mother," Lottie answered honestly. "But I think I'll stay home today."

"That may be best for once," Mother decided.

Lottie could hardly keep from smiling. Her plan was working!

After the family left, Lottie put on a pinafore to protect her dress. She picked up the basket of keys from her mother's room, took Mandy with her, and went out to the kitchen. Mandy called in her husband and young son to help.

First, they built a fire in the stove and fireplace. Lottie made cookies and set them aside to cool. She sent the men to the orchard for peaches and to the garden for tomatoes and corn. Mandy made the necessary trips to the spring and to the smokehouse for meat.

"What fun this is," Lottie exclaimed as she mixed dough for hot biscuits.

"What will your mother do to us?" Mandy wondered as she peeled and sliced peaches for dessert. But she, too, was having a good time. Anything Lottie did was all right with her.

About the time the family was due back from the nearly twenty-mile-round-trip to church, the table was set with the family's finest tablecloth, china, and silver. And the food had been carried from the kitchen to the dining room smoking hot.

Just then the family carriage turned off the highway into the lane to the great-house. As Mrs. Moon looked toward home she exclaimed in alarm, "Is that smoke from our kitchen chimney?"

"Yes, it is," the coachman replied.

"Then hurry the horses as fast as you can," she urged. "Oh, I do hope the kitchen is not on fire!"

As the coach stopped in front of the house, Mrs. Moon rushed toward the kitchen. But she stopped short, for there was Lottie busily making gravy for the chicken.

"Whatever are you doing?" Mother asked in a shocked voice. "So this is why you wanted to stay home!" And before

28

Lottie could answer, Mother turned and walked quickly to the house.

The food Lottie had cooked was delicious. But the family ate it in silence.

When the meal was over, Mrs. Moon asked Lottie to remain. "I am disappointed in you," Mother began. "You have broken our rules for keeping the sabbath. And you have disobeyed me. You must go to your room and stay until I send for you. You will eat bread and milk till then."

With this Mrs. Moon dismissed Lottie and turned her face toward the windows that looked out on the blue hills far away. She missed her husband more than ever at times like these.

Lottie went to her room slowly.

All that afternoon, that night, and the next day she thought and thought about what she had done.

"I should not have made Mother unhappy," she decided. "But why is it wrong to cook on Sunday? And why do I have to go to church just because the family does? Why are the sermons so long to me and so short and interesting to Mother? I wish I knew!"

Late the next day Mother sent word for Lottie to join her in the study.

"I'm sorry I made you sad, Mother," Lottie apologized. "You won't see any more 'sabbath smoke' rise from our kitchen chimney. I promise. And I'll try to go to church everytime you do."

"Thank you, Lottie," Mother answered with love in her voice. "I know you will keep your word. But someday, I hope you go to church because you like to sing, to pray, and to hear about God."

"I'll try, Mother. I really will try."

5
The Silent Bell

Life at Viewmont was never dull for Lottie.

She studied her lessons, practiced the piano, sewed, helped weave cloth, knitted, cooked, or read. She also took walks with her favorite dog out over the hills and through the woods on the backside of the plantation.

And she teased everybody and played jokes on them.

"You are a joy, Lottie, even though you do play too many pranks on us at times," her mother often told her.

When Lottie was fourteen, the governess told Mrs. Moon, "I have taught

Lottie all I can. She likes to study, and I think you should send her to a school for higher learning, just as you have sent Thomas and Oriana."

"I think so, too," answered Mrs. Moon. "I have already arranged for her to attend Valley Union Seminary near Roanoke just as soon as she is ready."

At once Mrs. Moon and Lottie began to prepare for Lottie's stay at the girl's boarding school. They made new dresses and bonnets, knitted stockings, sweaters, and gloves. And they had new shoes and boots made.

"When I'm gone," Lottie told her mother one day, "I will miss the children, especially little sister Edmonia. Mary, Isaac, and Sarah are dear ones, but Eddie is special because she is the youngest."

"We will miss you, too," Mother answered. "But you must go on. Your father would have wanted it."

"You have a keen mind and the ability to learn many things. God expects you to do your best. And I know you will."

"I'm not too sure about that," Lottie replied. "But I do like to read and study."

When everything was packed, Lottie started on the two-hundred-mile trip. She went to Charlottesville and rode the train from there to Roanoke. From Roanoke she went in a carriage to the valley

where the school was located. It snuggled among the hazy Blue Ridge Mountains of Virginia. "How beautiful!" she exclaimed as she looked from the school grounds to the mountains.

That night as Lottie went to sleep she thought, "I like it here. But how will I ever wake at six o'clock in the morning without Mandy?"

She should not have worried about it. The next morning she was frightened out of bed by a clanging, such as she had heard but few times in her life. At Viewmont they rang a bell like this only when there was a fire or awful accident.

"What has happened?" she cried. "Is the building on fire?" And she grabbed her robe as she started for the door.

"No, no," several of her roommates answered as they raised their heads to see what this new girl was doing.

"That is only the rising bell," one explained. "In thirty minutes we are to be ready to attend daily worship, and at seven we will eat breakfast."

Lottie began to dress. "I do not like that loud bell," she decided right then.

All winter and early spring Lottie waked with a start when the rising bell clanged. **1571083**

"If I could just sleep late one morning, or wake to a quieter sound, I think I would not mind so," she kept telling herself. "I wonder how I could silence that bellclapper?"

Finally, she climbed up the belltower to have a look. This helped her think of a scheme, but she did not dare tell anyone about it.

On the night before April Fool's Day, Lottie lay awake until she felt sure everyone in the building was asleep. Then she crept out of bed, took towels and sheets, and went quietly in the dark, up the ladder to the bell.

Without a sound she tied the sheets

and towels around the bellclapper. "There!" she whispered happily, "no loud noise will scare us awake to-morrow. And what a good April Fool's trick to play on everyone!"

Lottie returned to bed and to sleep.

When the sexton pulled the bell rope the next morning at six, no sound came. He kept pulling the rope, but still with-out success. Finally, he gave up and waited.

About an hour later Headmaster Cocke waked and learned that not only he, but the whole school had overslept.

"What happened to the bell?" he asked the sexton.

"I haven't found out, sir. It just will not ring," was the reply.

When Mr. Cocke found out that Lottie had played the joke, he lectured her on proper and improper conduct.

At the end of the term, she did not get a conduct grade. "You do not deserve one," was the reason given.

Lottie worried a little about it. "Mother was right about reaping what you sow," she sighed. "And she will grieve over this. I wonder why I don't like to follow rules as others seem to? And why is it bad to play jokes on others? I will have to find the answers to these questions," she decided. "But how and where?"

6
Lottie Finds the Answer

Lottie completed three years of study at Hollins Institute. This was the new name for Union Valley Seminary for Girls.

Then she returned to Viewmont to decide what she should do next.

Mother had an idea. "A new school for women has been opened in Charlottesville," she explained. "It offers the same kind of education to women that the University of Virginia offers to men. Would you like to go there?"

"Yes, I surely would," Lottie replied. "I want to find out many things for myself. However," she added, "I do not yet know what I will do when I finish."

"You can pray about it as you prepare," Mother advised. "There will be plenty of time to decide within the next three years."

"I hope so," said Lottie.

To herself she thought, "But I'm not interested in praying about it. How could that help?"

Within a few days Lottie was ready to load her trunk and leave for school. The servants brought the carriage to the side door, loaded her belongings, and helped her in. Away she bounced and bumped and jostled over the ten miles of road to Charlottesville.

At the school Lottie told the director, "I want to learn French, German, and Spanish, as well as the subjects you think I should study. But I am most interested in Latin and Greek."

"You may follow such a course," she was told.

Lottie, along with her regular studies, read all kinds of books. She learned about the peoples of Europe, Africa, India. She read about Burma where the Judsons had gone many years before as missionaries. She studied the religions of all these people.

However, she did not yet have a religion of her own. Nor did she like to go to church any better now than she did when she was twelve.

One Monday she said to a friend who never missed church and often invited Lottie to go with her: "Now, now! I had a better time yesterday out on the haystack reading Shakespeare than you did going to that stuffy old church."

On another day during the year, one of her friends asked her to attend revival services in the school chapel. "You will like to hear Dr. Broadus," explained the friend. "He is a real Bible scholar."

"I've heard him before at church in

town," Lottie replied with a smile. "He won't say anything I'm interested in hearing."

Another friend invited her to a prayer meeting for the same revival. "What is there to pray about?" Lottie asked in a joking manner.

"Yourself," was the kind reply. "Lottie, we are praying with Dr. Broadus that you will let Jesus be the one to guide you all your life."

"And what interest is it of yours how I

spend my life?" Lottie answered shortly.

She turned away and said to herself, "I have not asked them to pray for me!" And the more she thought about it, the more she resented it.

"I will go to church tonight," she decided, "and prove that what they have, I do not need."

That night she walked into the service with her head high and an amused look on her face. But the smile faded when she saw girls look at one another and seem pleased that she had come.

"They will not be so happy tomorrow when I have finished making fun of all that happens here tonight," she mused.

But as Dr. Broadus began to explain how Jesus can help his followers live a happy, useful life, Lottie began to listen. She forgot why she had come to the service. She forgot the girls around her.

"Can Jesus answer all my questions about how to live everyday?" she wondered. "Can he help me want to obey rules? Will I like going to church if I follow his teachings? Can he give me peace in my heart?"

After the service she slipped away to her room, very troubled indeed. She didn't sleep much that night.

As the sun rose the next morning, Lottie for the first time joined the other girls in the special prayer meeting. "I have come to be one of you," she explained happily. "I have decided to follow Jesus for life."

From that day on Lottie began to study the Bible. She even read the New Testament in its original language, Greek.

"Lottie has changed," her friends said to one another. "She is still a lot of fun. She jokes and plays tricks on us," they added. "But she is careful not to hurt anyone's feelings with what she does."

"She isn't restless like she used to be

either," another good friend added.

And Lottie decided, "Jesus is really the answer to my questions. I have deep satisfaction in my heart at last. And I will play no more jokes that are unkind to others."

7
Lottie Makes
Cookies Again

The War Between the States began the summer Lottie finished college at Charlottesville. And when the war was over, four years later, Lottie's family had lost most of their wealth. Their many slaves had been set free.

"I don't mind about the money," Lottie thought. "And no one should make slaves of other men and women. But I'm glad we did not lose Viewmont!"

After a while Lottie decided to teach. She helped start a girls' school in Cartersville, Georgia.

School had barely begun when she was called home because of her mother's serious illness and death.

"What will you do now?" Edmonia asked Lottie as they discussed their future.

"I shall go back to Cartersville to teach," was the answer. "And what will you do?"

"I want to go North China," Edmonia replied. "They need a single woman to teach there."

"I have often thought of going to China or Burma," Lottie added. "I have thought of it since Mother read us the story of the Judsons many years ago. But I'm not sure yet what I should do. Until I know, I will teach school in this country."

Edmonia did go to Teng Chow, North China. And Lottie enjoyed her stay in Cartersville. She taught young people both in school and at Sunday School.

One Sunday in February of 1873, Lottie went to church as she always did, now.

She listened to the pastor preach as she always did, now. She heard him make this plea: "Young people are needed to take the gospel of Jesus to other lands. Is there one here today who will go?"

And Lottie made up her mind. She walked down the aisle, and explained to the minister and the people present, "God wants me in China, and I am ready to go."

Lottie left Viewmont in August of that year. She rode a train to California, boarded a ship in San Francisco, and sailed to Shanghai, China. From there she took a small ship north five hundred miles to Chefoo. A few days later she entered Teng Chow in a mule litter, called a "shentza."

"What a long, long trip," she told Edmonia. "There was a storm on the way over, and I thought I would die of seasickness. But the ride in the mule litter from Chefoo was the roughest I have ever had in my life!"

Lottie began at once to learn the strange language of the people. They used pictures for words instead of spelling with letters. And they read from the back of a book forward. The lines ran from top to bottom and began on the right side of the page. But Lottie found it interesting and loved to study it.

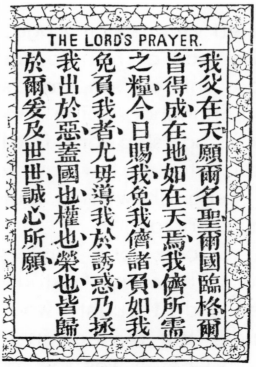

THE LORD'S PRAYER.

我父在天願爾名聖爾國臨格爾
旨得成在地如在天焉我儕所需
之糧今日賜我免我儕諸負如我
免負我者尤毋導我於誘惑乃拯
我出於惡蓋國也權也榮也皆歸
於爾爰及世世誠心所願

THE LORD'S PRAYER IN CHINESE.

She and Edmonia started a school for girls. Few came that first year. "You see," Mrs. Holmes, an older missionary, explained to the sisters, "the Chinese parents do not think girls can learn as boys do."

Before long Edmonia became ill. She grew worse, and Lottie decided to go with her back to their home in Virginia.

However, Lottie returned to Teng Chow on Christmas Eve, 1877.

"I am glad to get back here to North China," she wrote home. "I have received a warm welcome. But best of all I have found a house at an important street crossing. We call my new home 'Shao-Shi-Tsi-Ko', which means 'The Little Cross Roads.'"

For several years Miss Moon lived there and taught boys and girls the Bible and how to read and write.

One day Lottie heard that some of the Chinese at Ping-tu worshiped one god instead of many. "They should learn Bible truths easily," she said to the missionary, Dr. Crawford. "I would like to go there."

"They do not even like for foreign men to come to that area," he objected. "So I am sure it would be too dangerous for a single foreign woman to travel the hundred miles there alone. And on the way you would have to go through Laichofu (Li-chow-foo). They kill or imprison every foreigner who enters their city."

But the more Miss Moon thought of it, the more she felt she should go.

"I will not be by myself," she argued. "God will be with me. He will show me a safe way through the city. I feel I must go."

Before long Lottie loaded a shentza and left.

When she neared the city of Laichofu, the drivers asked, "How can we get

through without trouble, Miss Moon?"

"I have prayed and thought about it," she said. "Let's muffle the bells on the donkeys with hay. And when it gets dark, let's go through silently. In the blackness no one can see that I am a woman or a foreigner."

This is what they did. They went through without harm.

Miss Moon settled in Ping-tu to stay for a long time. She invited the women to her home. But they came slowly.

She tried to get the children from the street to come into her courtyard. She offered them cookies made by the recipes learned long ago from her mother. But the children would run away.

"She wishes to poison us," they said to each other. "She is a foreign devil!"

Miss Moon did not give up. She kept baking cookies until finally one little boy ate them because he was so hungry. No harm came to him. He didn't even get sick!

After that, all the children in the neighborhood came to eat the cookies. And they became friends with Miss Moon. They followed her through the streets. They listened as she told stories about Jesus. They even learned to sing "Jesus Loves Me"—in Chinese, of course.

8
An Important
Letter

After Miss Moon had worked for many months in Ping-tu, she wrote to the Foreign Mission Board in Richmond, Virginia. "I am the only missionary to thousands in this area. And I am a seven-day-journey from Teng Chow. Won't you please send at least two women to help me?"

"We do not have the money it would take," Dr. Tupper of the Board wrote back.

Miss Moon worked on.

Finally, she went back to Teng Chow to spend a few months with the missionaries there. "I am so lonely in Ping-tu, and there is too much for one missionary to do," she explained to her friends. "I am very tired after ten years work here in China."

To Dr. Tupper she wrote again, "I feel I must come to the United States for a rest."

"You may come," was his reply.

But on a Sunday before she could get ready, two men knocked on her door. "We are from Ping-tu," they told her. "The women and children there sent us to find you. They have waited a long time for your return. They need you there to help them."

With a thrill Miss Moon thought, "At last they think of me as their friend! Now they will listen to what I have to tell them about God."

And to the men she said, "I will come to Ping-tu as soon as I can get ready. I want to help your people."

To Dr. Tupper she wrote a letter like:

```
Dear Dr. Tupper:

        There is no one to take my place in
Ping-tu.  So I will not leave here yet.  Can't
you send just two women to work in my
place while I come home?

        Why can't the Baptists in the South
give a special Christmas offering for
missions as the Methodist women are
doing?

                            Sincerely,

                            Lottie Moon
```

When Dr. Tupper received the letter at the Foreign Mission Board in Richmond, he handed it to Miss Annie Armstrong who was visiting from Baltimore. She was helping Baptist women of the South organize mission bands in their churches.

Miss Armstrong read the letter from Miss Moon and then asked, "Dr. Tupper, do you think the Baptist women would give enough money to send two missionaries to Ping-tu?"

"Ask them and see," he replied.

And Miss Armstrong did. She sent letters to the women in churches all over the South. She explained why Miss Moon did not come home for a much needed rest. She asked them to give a special offering for China at Christmas time.

"Will they give?" she kept asking herself.

Then came Christmas! The women did give. The children brought their offerings, too. When all the gifts were counted, Miss Armstrong could hardly believe the total amount.

Dr. Tupper wrote the good news to Miss Moon. "You can come home now. We have received more than enough money to send the two women to take your place."

Miss Lottie was overjoyed. But, of course, she didn't leave at once. "I will stay until the young ladies get here," she answered Dr. Tupper. "And won't you send a preacher, too?"

Miss Moon did stay. She worked three more years in Ping-tu. The two ladies came as promised and began to learn Chinese and the work. Then a minister moved to the city with his wife.

"I can go home to Virginia now," said Miss Moon.

On New Year's Day, 1891, after almost fourteen years, Miss Lottie saw Viewmont again and the beautiful Blue Ridge Mountains beyond.

"It is good to be home again!" she told her sister Edmonia.

"It is good to be home again," she wrote Miss Armstrong. "Please thank the women and children for their Christmas gifts that made it possible."

Miss Moon returned to China after her visit to Virginia. But she did not go to Ping-tu to live.

Four missionaries had taken her place. She was glad that they had come.

She reopened her home, "The Little Cross Roads," in Teng Chow. And there she lived and worked for the rest of her life.

The Chinese people no longer called her "Devil-Old-Woman," as they once did. She was their friend, "Moo La Dee, the Heavenly-Book-Visitor."

She visited them from house to house and told them about God's love. She taught them to read the Bible for themselves.

LOTTIE MOON AND CHINESE FRIENDS

Courtesy of The Southern Baptist Theological Seminary

9
The Lottie Moon Christmas Offering

Lottie Moon died on Christmas Eve, 1912. She was 72 years old and had spent nearly 40 years in China.

The Baptist women of the South continued to give a special mission offering at Christmas, as she had suggested years before.

"Let's name the offering for the one who gave us the idea," the women said in 1918, as they met in Hot Springs, Arkansas. "Let's call it the 'Lottie Moon Christmas Offering' for Christ."

This is how the offering taken in Baptist churches every year at Christmas got its name.

The first offering was for missions in China only. It amounted to more than $3,000.

The offerings today come not only from the women and children but from all Southern Baptist church members. This money is used for mission work around the world. It helps to build churches, hospitals, schools, and to send preachers, doctors, nurses, teachers, and many other kinds of Christian workers. The gift adds up to millions of dollars at Christmas time.